Best Easy Day Hikes
Berkshires

Help Us Keep This Guide Up to Date

Every effort has been made by the author and editors to make this guide as accurate and useful as possible. However, many things can change after a guide is published—trails are rerouted, regulations change, facilities come under new management, etc.

We would appreciate hearing from you concerning your experiences with this guide and how you feel it could be improved and kept up to date. While we may not be able to respond to all comments and suggestions, we'll take them to heart and we'll also make certain to share them with the author. Please send your comments and suggestions to the following address:

GPP
Reader Response/Editorial Department
P.O. Box 480
Guilford, CT 06437

Or you may e-mail us at:

editorial@GlobePequot.com

Thanks for your input, and happy trails!

Best Easy Day Hikes Series

Best Easy Day Hikes
Berkshires

Jim Bradley

FALCON GUIDES

GUILFORD, CONNECTICUT
HELENA, MONTANA

AN IMPRINT OF GLOBE PEQUOT PRESS

FALCONGUIDES®

Layout: Kevin Mak
Project editor: Gregory Hyman
Maps by Mapping Specialists © Morris Book Publishing, LLC

TOPO! Explorer software and SuperQuad source maps courtesy of National Geographic Maps. For information about TOPO! Explorer, TOPO!, and Nat Geo Maps products, go to www.topo.com or www.natgeomaps.com.

Library of Congress Cataloging-in-Publication data is available on file.

ISBN 978-0-7627-6057-2

Printed in the United States of America

10 9 8 7 6 5 4 3 2 1

Contents

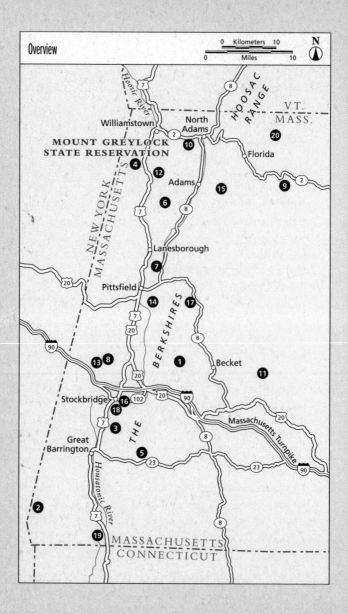

Acknowledgments

I would like to thank the many rangers and local hikers that were happy to answer questions and listen to me ramble on. Thanks to the many land conservation groups for protecting land and making it available for outdoor recreation. Thanks to friends and family for their continued support and encouragement. A very special thanks to Lisa O'Brien: I would have been lost without her love and support.

Introduction

The Berkshires are located in the far west section of Massachusetts, in the rolling hills between New York and Boston. Well known for their natural beauty and ease of access, the Berkshires have inspired great authors and artists such as Nathaniel Hawthorne, Norman Rockwell, Herman Melville, and Henry David Thoreau over the years.

The Appalachian Mountains run north–south through the region, locally known as the Berkshire Hills. The Taconic Range cuts into the northwest corner of the area and contains Massachusetts's highest peak, Mount Greylock (3,491 feet). If you are willing to put the work in, hiking in either of these ranges affords some marvelous views. Don't think the beauty ends there: The Hoosic River and the Housatonic River run through valleys in the Berkshires, a backdrop for possibly more gorgeous scenery than the mountaintops. Many would say to save your trip for peak fall foliage in autumn, when the hills explode with color, but beauty can be found in any season!

The Mahican (muh-he-ka-neew) Native American tribe originally inhabited the area, until the early 1700s when English settlers bought the land from the tribe. In the early 1800s the American elite started building cottages on the hillsides, because the hilly terrain of the Berkshires was not sought after by farmers (although some tried to farm the rocky mountainsides). As the iron industry grew in the late eighteenth and early nineteenth centuries, logging started to become the norm in the Berkshires. Many hillsides were stripped of timber, leaving trees in only the hardest to reach areas.

Today, the Berkshires offer a cultural focal point for historic sites, art, museums, dance, and music venues such as Jacob's Pillow Dance Festival; MASS MoCA, the country's largest contemporary art center; Tanglewood, the summer home of the Boston Symphony Orchestra; and the Norman Rockwell Museum, just to name a few. Arts and culture come second to outdoor recreation, with opportunities for hiking, backpacking, bicycling, fishing, boating, cross-country and alpine skiing, and hunting scattered all throughout the Berkshires.

The Berkshires seem to have the right balance of small picturesque towns, arts, and protected natural beauty through land conservation. Pittsfield is the largest city in the Berkshires, with a population of around 42,000 people. Some of the smaller towns of the Berkshires, such as Monroe and Mount Washington, have fewer than one hundred residents. The Massachusetts Department of Conservation and Recreation protects and maintains about twenty-five properties, totaling over 115,000 acres, in the Berkshires. Numerous private land-conservation groups also maintain a large number of properties in the area. Hiking and outdoor recreation is strongly supported in the Berkshires.

The Nature of the Berkshires

Berkshires' trails range from the rugged and hilly to the flat and paved. Hikes in this guide cover the full spectrum. While by definition a best easy day hike is not strenuous and poses little danger to the traveler, knowing a few details about the nature of the area will enhance your explorations.

Weather

The Berkshires are quite a bit hillier than the rest of the state. Therefore, the weather is a bit more dramatic. You might hear locals say "If you don't like the weather, wait ten minutes." This is a bit of a stretch, but strange weather is not uncommon in the Berkshires.

The best weather for hiking is in summer and fall, when high temperatures range from the 40s to the 80s and the spring thaw has passed, allowing the wet trails to dry up. Winter snowmelt and heavy spring rains saturate many area trails, leaving them muddy. Hiking on muddy trails promotes erosion, which in turn creates more muddy trails.

An average of 36 inches of rain falls in the area annually, mostly in spring and early summer. Snowfall averages 70 inches annually, and can remain on the ground well into April, especially at higher elevations and heavily shaded areas. Winter lows can plunge into the negatives, but winter daytime highs are usually in the 20s. When hiking in winter, wear layers of clothing, a hat, and gloves to insulate you from the cold and potential rain or snow.

Summertime temperatures are not oppressive, with averages in the 70s and 80s. In fall, the leaves start to change as the temperature drops; expect temperatures in the 40s, 50s, and 60s in fall months. Peak fall foliage usually happens in the beginning of October but changes year to year.

Critters

You will encounter mostly benign creatures on these trails, such as squirrels, rabbits, turkeys, and a variety of birdlife. More rarely seen are coyotes, deer, moose, bobcat, and black bear. Encounters with wildlife that pose a potential threat to hikers are very rare but are definitely possible, so beware the venomous snake, black bear, moose, and bobcat.

Massachusetts is home to only two species of venomous snakes, the timber rattlesnake and the copperhead. These snakes are so rare hikers rarely see them. You can find twelve other snake species in Massachusetts, all harmless. The most common snake encounter will be with the garter snake, which can be recognized by its pattern of yellow stripes on a black or brown background. Snakes generally only strike if they are threatened—you are too big to be dinner, so they typically avoid contact with humans. Keep your distance, and they will keep theirs. If you encounter a snake on the trail, give it space.

Black bear encounters usually involve some kind of food, whether left in a car, a tent, a garbage can, or on a windowsill. They've been known to remove windshields from automobiles to get at coolers and to stroll into homes when the doors are left open to rummage in refrigerators. If you encounter a bear on the trail, do not run. Stand still, make noise, and the bear will generally scram. Never come between a mama bear and her cubs; if you see cubs, leave the area immediately!

The biggest nuisances of the woods are ticks and mosquitoes. Ticks are an arachnid found in tall grass, shrubs, and trees waiting to attach to a passing host. Ticks can transmit both Lyme disease and Rocky Mountain spotted fever. In order to transmit a disease the tick must remain attached for twenty-four to forty-eight hours, so it is very important to do a thorough check for ticks when returning from a hike. Mosquitoes are flying insects capable of drinking blood. The site of a mosquito bite becomes welted, red, and itchy. Even though mosquitoes can transmit disease, the chances are low in this region. Your best defense against pests including ticks and mosquitoes is using an insect repellant containing at least 30 percent deet. Spray on your clothing, especially on cuffs and your waistline, avoiding contact with your skin. Do not use products containing deet on young children.

Safety and Preparation

Hikers' checklist:
- Notify someone of your plans
- A backpack or fanny pack
- Water
- Snack food
- Knife
- First-aid kit
- Map and compass or GPS unit
- Insect repellant and sunscreen
- Fire starter/matches

Hikers should be prepared for any situation, whether they are out for a short stroll or an all day adventure.
- Know the basics of first aid, including how to treat bleeding, bites and stings, and fractures, strains, and sprains. Pack a first-aid kit on each excursion.
- Regardless of the weather, your body needs a lot of water while hiking. Consuming a full twenty-ounce bottle is the minimum for short hikes. You will need more for a longer hike. A good rule of thumb is eight to ten ounces per mile.

- Don't drink from streams, rivers, creeks, or lakes without treating or filtering the water first. Waterways and water bodies may host a variety of contaminants, including giardia, which can cause serious intestinal unrest.

- Prepare for extremes of both heat and cold by dressing in layers.

- Carry a backpack in which you can store extra clothing, ample drinking water and food, and whatever goodies, like guidebooks, cameras, and binoculars, you might want.

- Cell phone coverage in the Berkshires is spotty at best. Bring your device, but make sure you've turned it off or got it on the vibrate setting while hiking. No need to annoy everyone within earshot with a loud phone ring. On longer hikes, turning off your phone also conserves the battery charge for use in case of emergency.

- Keep children under careful watch. Have them carry a plastic whistle: If they become lost, they should stay in one place and blow the whistle three times to summon help.

Hunting Season Safety

A large number of animals can be legally hunted in Massachusetts. Many of the properties listed in this guide allow hunting. Hunting is a year-round sport in the Berkshires; most often hunters enter the woods in late fall and early spring for deer and turkey seasons. No hunting is allowed in any season on Sunday in the state. Check with the Commonwealth of Massachusetts Division of Wildlife and Fisheries for hunting season information (www.mass.gov /dfwele).

During peak hunting seasons, it is a good idea to wear bright colors and stay on marked trails. Massachusetts law requires hunters to wear at least 500 square inches of blaze orange when in the woods, a good rule for hikers to follow too. Taking a few precautions can allow for safe hiking even during peak seasons.

Leave No Trace

Trails in the Berkshires are heavily used; some can see ten thousand or more visitors a year. We, as trail users and advocates, must be especially vigilant to make sure our passage leaves no lasting mark. Here are some basic guidelines for preserving trails in the region:

- Pack out all your own trash, including biodegradable items like orange and banana peels. You might also pack out garbage left by less-considerate hikers.
- Avoid damaging trailside soils and plants by remaining on the established route. Social trails created by hikers, cyclists, and off-road vehicles are a plague on area parklands, contributing to erosion problems and creating unsightly scars on the landscape. Don't cut switchbacks, which can promote erosion.
- Don't approach or feed any wild creatures—the squirrel eyeing your snack food is best able to survive if it remains self-reliant.
- Don't pick wildflowers or gather rocks, antlers, feathers, and other treasures along the trail. Removing these items will only take away from the experience of the next hiker.
- Be courteous by not making loud noises while hiking.

- Many of these trails are multiuse, which means you'll share them with other hikers, trail runners, mountain bikers, and equestrians. Familiarize yourself with the proper trail etiquette, yielding the trail when appropriate. The general rule is, cyclists should yield to hikers and horses, and hikers yield to horses. Most times, it is easier for a hiker to step aside rather than a biker. I personally think this is safer and recommend it.
- Use outhouses at trailheads or along the trail.

Emergency Care

Hospitals
- North Adams Regional Hospital, 71 Hospital Ave., North Adams; (413) 664-5000; www.nbhealth.org
- Fairview Hospital, 29 Lewis Ave., Great Barrington; (413) 528-0790; www.berkshirehealthsystems.org/body_fh.cfm?id=39
- Berkshire Medical Center, 725 North St., Pittsfield; (413) 447-2000; www.berkshirehealthsystems.org/body_bmc.cfm?id=43

Twenty-Four-Hour Veterinary Care
Berkshire Veterinary Hospital, 730½ Crane Ave., Pittsfield; (413) 499-2820; www.berkshirevet.com

Land Management

The following agencies manage most of the public lands described in this guide and can provide further information on these hikes and other trails in their service areas.

- Massachusetts Department of Conservation and Recreation, 251 Causeway St., Suite 600, Boston 02114-2104; (617) 626-1250; www.mass.gov/dcr
- The Trustees of Reservations, The Mission House, P.O. Box 792/1 Sergeant St., Stockbridge 01262; (413) 298-3239 ext. 3000; www.thetrustees.org
- Berkshire Natural Resources Council, 20 Bank Row, Pittsfield 01201; (413) 499-0596; www.bnrc.net
- Mass Audubon, 208 South Great Rd., Lincoln 01773; (781) 259-9500; www.massaudubon.org
- Commonwealth of Massachusetts Department of Fish and Game, 251 Causeway St. #400, Boston 02114; (617) 626-1500; www.mass.gov/dfwele

How to Use This Guide

This guide is designed to be simple and easy to use. Each hike is described with a map and summary information that delivers the trail's vital statistics including length, difficulty, fees and permits, park hours, canine compatibility, and trail contacts. Directions to the trailhead as well as the GPS coordinates of the parking area are also provided, along with a general description of what you'll see along the way. A detailed route finder (Miles and Directions) sets forth mileages between significant landmarks along the trail.

How the Hikes Were Chosen

This guide describes trails that are accessible to every hiker, whether visiting from out of town or a local resident. Most hikes are no longer than 6 miles round-trip, and most are considerably shorter, with an emphasis on interpretive nature trails. They range in difficulty from flat excursions perfect for a family outing to more challenging treks into the steep, rocky, high country of the Berkshires. While these trails are among the best, keep in mind that nearby trails, sometimes in the same park or in a neighboring open space, may offer options better suited to your needs.

Selecting a Hike

These are all easy hikes, but easy is a relative term. Some would argue that no hike involving any kind of climbing is easy, but climbs are a fact of life in the Berkshires.

- **Easy** hikes are generally short and flat, taking no longer than an hour or two to complete.

- **Moderate** hikes involve increased distance and relatively mild changes in elevation, and will take two hours or more to complete.
- **More challenging** hikes feature some long climbs, steep stretches, and greater distances.

Keep in mind that what you think is easy is entirely dependent on your level of fitness and the adequacy of your gear (primarily shoes). Use the trail's length as a gauge of its relative difficulty—even if climbing is involved, it won't be bad if the hike is less than 1 mile long. If you are hiking with a group, select a hike that is appropriate for the least fit and prepared person in your party.

Approximate hiking times are based on the assumption that on flat ground, most walkers average 2 miles per hour. Adjust that rate by the steepness of the terrain and your level of fitness (subtract time if you're an aerobic animal and add time if you're hiking with kids), and you have a ballpark hiking duration. Be sure to add more time if you plan to picnic or take part in other activities like bird watching or photography.

Trail Finder

Best Hikes for Beginners

Best Hikes for Waterfalls

Best Hikes for Great Views

Best Hikes for History Lovers

Best Hikes for Children

Best Hikes for Dogs

Best Hikes for Birders

Map Legend

35	Interstate Highway
6	U.S. Highway
92	State Highway
	Local Road
	Unpaved Road
	Railroad
	Featured Trail
	Trail
	State Line
	Boardwalk/Steps
	River/Creek
	Marsh/Swamp
	Body of Water
	Local/State Park
	Local/State Forest
⌣	Bridge
⛺	Camping
	Gate
▲	Mountain/Peak
🅿	Parking
🎪	Picnic Area
■	Point of Interest/Structure
	Restrooms
	Tower
○	Town
11	Trailhead
	Viewpoint/Overlook
❷	Visitor/Information Center
⋛	Waterfall

1 Washington Mountain Marsh

Hike around a defunct reservoir–turned–marsh. Zigzag around Washington Mountain Marsh on hundreds of feet of plank walkways and wooden bridges; pass within feet of active beaver dams, and see fine examples of the huts in which beavers live. October Mountain State Forest is Massachusetts's largest state forest at 16,500 acres.

Distance: 3.1-mile lollipop
Approximate hiking time: 1 to 2 hours
Trail surface: Gravel trail, forested trail, plank walkways
Difficulty: Easy
Best seasons: Summer and fall
Other trail users: Hikers only
Canine compatibility: Leashed dogs permitted
Fees and permits: None

Schedule: Open daily year-round, from sunrise to one half-hour after sunset
Maps: USGS East Lee; park map available at October Mountain Campground and on the park website
Trail contact: October Mountain State Forest, 256 Woodland Rd., Lee 01238; (413) 243-1778; www.mass.gov/dcr/parks/western/octm.htm

Finding the trailhead: From the MA 8 and US 20 intersection southeast of Pittsfield, take MA 8/Main Street north for 4.9 miles. Turn left at McNerney Road. In 100 feet make a slight left onto Country Road. Continue on Country Road (partially a dirt road and not plowed in winter) for 4.6 miles. At the Y, turn right onto Lenox-Whitney Place Road (dirt) and continue for 1.2 miles. At the four-way intersection turn left onto West Branch Road (dirt) and go 0.5 mile to the parking area and trailhead on the left. GPS: N42 21.163' / W73 11.276'

The Hike

From the parking area head north, crossing West Branch Road, to the signed trailhead. The first 800 feet of the trail is hard-packed gravel. Along the gravel section you pass an eighteenth-century cemetery to the right. Turn right at the junction and follow the blue-marked trail that will lead you around the marsh.

Almost every topographic map shows this body of water as Washington Mountain Lake. The strange thing is that this was never a lake. A leaky dam in a failed flood-control project prevented the lake from ever being formed, resulting in the marsh that exists today.

As the trail meets the marsh's edge, turn right at the sign to follow the outer loop. Part of the Interpretive Trail is closed due to flooding; at times of high water parts of the outer loop can flood but remain passable. As you make your way along the Outer Loop Trail you'll cross the marsh on many plank walkways. Cattails thrive in the marshy water along much of the trip. The trip around the marsh offers views of three excellent beaver dams almost within arms' reach.

At 2.2 miles pass the third and last beaver dam, with beaver huts in the backdrop. Keep straight at the sign for the Interpretive Trail; the Outer Loop Trail now merges with the Interpretive Trail and enters into the forest. The trail winds away from the marsh, meeting up with Knob Loop. Turn left to avoid Knob Loop and descend to the water's edge. You will cross the marsh one last time on a very long plank walkway, then meet back up with the gravel trail. Follow the trail straight back to the parking area and trailhead.

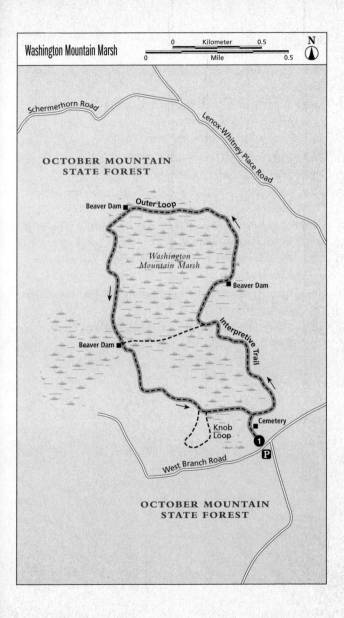

Miles and Directions

0.0 Start the hike across from the parking area off West Branch Road.

0.1 Turn right onto the Outer Loop Trail/Interpretive Trail and follow the blue trail markers.

0.8 Turn right at the sign for the Outer Loop Trail.

1.0 Arrive at the first beaver dam.

1.7 Arrive at the second beaver dam.

2.2 Arrive at the last beaver dam; notice the beaver huts in the background.

2.3 Keep straight onto Outer Loop/Interpretive Trail at the sign for the Interpretive Trail.

2.7 Turn left to keep on Outer Loop/Interpretive Trail at sign for Knob Loop.

3.0 Keep right on the gravel trail; follow the trail back toward the parking area.

3.1 Finish at the trailhead and parking area off West Branch Road.

2 Bash Bish Falls

Bash Bish Falls is a quick hike with a huge reward. Some say the 60-foot uninterrupted falls are Massachusetts's most spectacular. The Bash Bish Brook cascades nearly 120 feet before making the 20-foot plunge to the stone pillar that splits the falls into two, with both then dropping nearly 60 feet to the pool below.

Distance: 0.8 mile out and back
Approximate hiking time: 1 hour
Trail surface: Forested trail
Difficulty: Moderate
Best season: Spring
Other trail users: Bicyclists and snowshoers
Canine compatibility: Leashed dogs permitted
Fees and permits: None

Schedule: Open daily year-round, from sunrise to one half-hour after sunset
Maps: USGS Bash Bish Falls, MA, and Copake, NY; park map available on the park website
Trail contact: Mount Washington State Forest, 3 East St., Mount Washington 01258; (413) 528-0330; www.mass.gov/dcr/parks/western/bash.htm

Finding the trailhead: From the MA 23/MA 41 junction in South Egremont, take MA 41 (North Undermountain Road) south for 0.1 mile. Turn right onto Mount Washington Road; continue on Mount Washington Road for 4.4 miles. Turn right onto West Street. After 0.3 mile turn left to stay on West Street; continue on West Street for 1.7 miles. Turn right at Falls Road; continue on Falls Road for 1.4 miles to the upper parking area. GPS: N42 06.904' / W73 29.499'

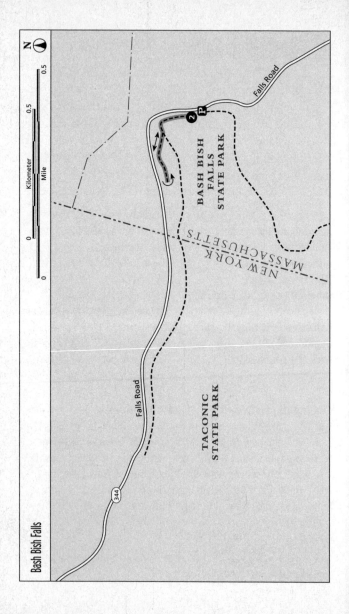

Bash Bish Falls

The Hike

The trail starts in the northwest corner of the parking area and descends quickly, passing an information kiosk that warns of a 300-foot elevation drop in 0.25 mile. The trail to the falls is marked in blue.

Cross an intermittent stream on a log bridge. At the bridge, the trail bends sharply to the left, descending steeply. At 0.3 mile the trail makes a sharp left, heading down to the access road. At the access road turn left, and the falls will be within sight. If you continue past the fenced viewing area, you can head down the man-made stone stairway to the base of the falls at 0.4 mile.

Climbing and swimming around the falls is prohibited. AOL Travel named Bash Bish Falls one of the top ten most dangerous travel destinations. The falls have claimed the lives of more than twenty-five people, but if the rules and regulations are followed Bash Bish is as safe as any other hike in this book.

The falls are named for a beautiful Indian woman called Bash Bish. Legend has it that Bash Bish was accused of adultery and the tribe elders sentenced her to death. She was to be tied to a canoe and turned loose upstream of the falls. As she and the canoe plunged into the falls, rays of sun formed a halo around her body and a swarm of butterflies flew around her. The canoe smashed to pieces at the base of the falls but no trace of Bash Bish's body was ever found. This haunted villagers for many years.

After enjoying the cooling mist at the base of the falls, retrace your route back to the upper parking area and trailhead.

Option

A flatter but longer hike to the falls begins at the New York State trailhead. The parking area for the New York side is 1 mile past the upper parking area on Falls Road. The trail follows the wide dirt access road, and heads southwest from the parking area. Keep straight on the access road to reach the falls. The round-trip distance for this route is 1.6 miles.

Miles and Directions

0.0 Start from the upper parking area off Falls Road.

0.3 Turn left onto the wide dirt road.

0.4 Arrive at Bash Bish Falls, then retrace your route to the upper parking area.

0.8 End your hike at the trailhead in the upper parking area off Falls Road.

3 Monument Mountain

Monument Mountain attracts over 20,000 visitors per year and it is no wonder why, given the awe-inspiring 360-degree views of the Taconic Range, Mount Greylock, and the Housatonic River valley. Well-marked trails take you to the summit of Squaw Peak, where you can have a picnic at the summit just like authors Nathaniel Hawthorne and Herman Melville did in 1850.

Distance: 2.7-mile loop
Approximate hiking time: 1 to 2 hours
Trail surface: Hard-packed forest floor, rock stairs
Difficulty: Moderate due to the climb to Squaw Peak
Best season: Fall
Other trail users: Trail runners, snowshoers, and cross-country skiers
Canine compatibility: Leashed dogs permitted

Fees and permits: Donation requested but no permit needed
Schedule: Open daily year-round, from sunrise to sunset
Maps: USGS Stockbridge; park map available on park website
Trail contact: The Trustees of Reservations, Berkshires, The Mission House, 1 Sergeant St., Stockbridge 01262; (413) 298-3239 ext. 3000; www.the trustees.org/places-to-visit/berk shires/monument-mountain.html

Finding the trailhead: From the intersection of MA 102 and US 7 in Stockbridge, take US 7 south for 3.0 miles to the trailhead parking area on the right. GPS: N42 14.596' / W73 20.124'

The Hike

From the map kiosk at the trailhead, head south on the well-marked Indian Monument Trail, traveling the loop in a clockwise direction. The trail follows the edge of US 7 for 0.5 mile before bending to the right and heading away from the roadway. As you climb Indian Monument Trail, the traffic noise fades. At the junction with Squaw Peak Trail, turn right onto Squaw Peak Trail. The trail to the Squaw Peak summit is steep and rocky in sections but the view is well worth the climb.

At 1.4 miles, pass a sign that reads SCENIC VISTA. Turn left to continue to the summit. **Side trip:** Turn right at the sign for a 0.1-mile round-trip to Devil's Pulpit, where you can stand atop white quartzite pillars and gaze west to the Taconic Range.

Squaw Peak's summit is 1,640 feet above sea level and offers an outstanding 360-degree view from the top of the quartzite mound at the high point. Mount Greylock, Massachusetts's highest peak, can be seen to the north. To the east look down onto Beartown State Forest; views to the west are of New York's Taconic Range.

From the summit continue north and start the very steep descent. Stone has been moved to create stairs to help make the climb down easier and prevent erosion. At Inscription Rock turn right onto Hickey Trail and continue the steep rocky descent.

At 2.0 miles, you will pass an unnamed waterfall. In the spring the 10-foot fall has good flow but this slows to a trickle as the summer dries it out. The trail follows along the edge of the small stream then bends left, heading away from the stream. As you get closer to the parking area, you will start to notice the US 7 traffic noise again.

Continue past a hillside of fallen quartzite boulders that have tumbled down from far above over the years, mostly due to cracks in the stone that filled with water and froze,

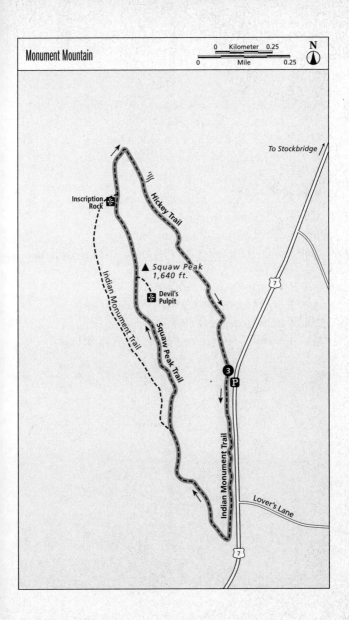

Monument Mountain

N

0   Kilometer   0.25
0   Mile   0.25

To Stockbridge

Hickey Trail

Inscription Rock

Indian Monument Trail

Squaw Peak
1,640 ft.

Devil's Pulpit

Squaw Peak Trail

3
P

Indian Monument Trail

Lover's Lane

7

7

splitting the rock. The trail gets wide and steep as you make the final descent to the parking area and trailhead.

Option

Forgo the steep climb to the Squaw Peak summit by keeping left on Indian Monument Trail at the junction with Squaw Peak Trail. Continue on Indian Monument Trail for 0.7 mile to Inscription Rock and Hickey Trail.

Miles and Directions

0.0   Start from the parking area off US 7.

0.9   Turn right onto the Squaw Peak Trail.

1.4   Turn left at the sign for the scenic vista to stay on the Squaw Peak Trail.

1.5   Arrive at the Squaw Peak summit.

1.7   Turn right onto the Hickey Trail at Inscription Rock.

2.0   Pass the unnamed waterfall.

2.7   Arrive back at the trailhead and parking area off US 7.

4 Field Farm

Field Farm is a 316-acre property owned and maintained by The Trustees of Reservations. Field Farm encompasses 4 miles of hiking trails through a working hayfield and pasture, offering up some of the best views of Mount Greylock and the Taconic Range. Roam through untouched forests to the small caves. This hike will take you to almost every corner of this great property.

Distance: 2.9-mile loop
Approximate hiking time: 1 to 2 hours
Trail surface: Grass paths and forested trails
Difficulty: Easy
Best seasons: Summer and fall
Other trail users: Trail runners, cross-country skiers, and snowshoers
Canine compatibility: Leashed dogs permitted

Fees and permits: Donation requested but no permit needed
Schedule: Open daily year-round, from sunrise to sunset
Maps: USGS Berlin; park map available on the park website
Trail contact: The Trustees of Reservations, Berkshires, The Mission House, 1 Sergeant St., Stockbridge 01262; (413) 298-3239 ext. 3000; www.thetrustees.org/places-to-visit/berkshires/field-farm.html

Finding the trailhead: From the intersection of US 7 and MA 43 in Williamstown, take MA 43 south for 200 feet. Take the first right onto Sloan Road, then continue on Sloan Road for 1.2 miles. Turn right at the sign for Field Farm and follow the signs for the parking area and trailhead. GPS: N42 39.930' / W73 15.624'

The Hike

Start the hike from the map kiosk by heading northeast on the Pond Trail. The trail cuts through the woods and quickly emerges at the pond. Turn right, keeping the water to your left and traveling the loop in a counterclockwise direction. Follow the edge of the pond and keep straight to North-South Trail.

At the hayfield turn right and follow the edge of the field. This is a working hayfield so expect to see farm equipment. At the break in the tree line cross over to the adjacent field and continue north. At the end of the field, turn slightly right onto the Oak Loop.

Although the trail is named for oaks, sugar maples make up a good portion of the forest surrounding the Oak Loop. At the junction with the Caves Trail, turn right to head to the caves. Caves Trail climbs to the top of a small ridge; from the ridgetop Mount Greylock can be seen through the tree cover. Descend the ridge and turn left, keeping on Caves Trail.

At 1.4 miles, you will arrive at the caves. These are not caves you would normally think of, with large mouths. Instead, small streams run into openings in the rocks and down to the caves. Most caves are of this type and go unnoticed. Throughout this section of trail, keep a lookout for small streams that seem to run to nowhere. In the winter, as the caves freeze, the streams back up and create a pond in the area. This pond slowly drains into the caves as they thaw in spring.

Continue past the caves and turn right onto the Oak Loop. Follow along a peaceful winding stream. When the trail enters the pasture, turn right onto North Trail. In just

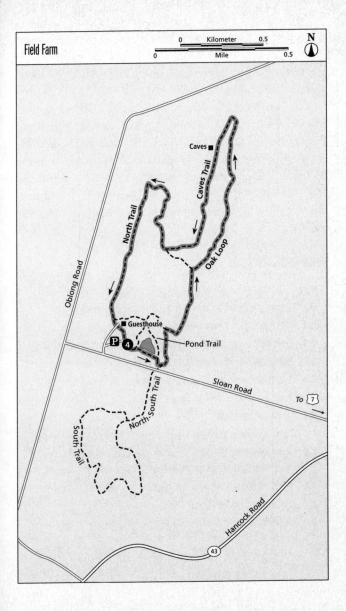

Field Farm

Kilometer
0   0.5
0   0.5
Mile

N

Caves ■

Caves Trail

North Trail

Oak Loop

Oblong Road

■ Guesthouse

P 4

Pond Trail

Sloan Road

To 7

North-South Trail

South Trail

Hancock Road

43

a few feet, you will see a sign for North Trail, which turns right, heading into the forest. The trail bends sharply to the left at the property line and continues through the forest heading back to the pasture.

At 2.5 miles, keep straight along the edge of the pasture. Magnificent views of Mount Greylock can be seen across the pasture to the northeast. The trail continues behind the guesthouse. Walk across the guesthouse lawn, crossing the driveway, and pass through the opening in the hedges. You will pass a group of art sculptures, then the trail continues through a small patch of trees back to the parking area and trailhead.

Miles and Directions

0.0   Start from the parking area off Sloan Road on Pond Trail.

0.1   Turn right to follow along the right side of the pond.

0.2   Stay straight to North-South Trail.

0.4   Turn right at the hayfield to keep on the North Trail.

0.7   Turn slightly right onto the Oak Loop.

0.9   Turn right onto the Caves Trail.

1.3   Turn left to stay on the Caves Trail.

1.4   Arrive at the caves.

1.7   Turn right onto the Oak Loop.

1.9   Turn right onto the North Trail at the pasture; in just a few feet turn right again and the North Trail enters the woods.

2.5   Keep straight, following the pasture's edge.

2.8   Cut through guesthouse yard.

2.9   Arrive back at the trailhead and parking area.

5 Pond Loop: Beartown State Forest

Hike around the 35-acre Benedict Pond, taking a rest half-way to sit on the bench gazing over the pond and listen to the children swim and play. This easy-to-follow flat hike is great for beginners or hikers with young children. Possible wildlife sightings include deer, bobcat, beaver, and bear, to name a few.

Distance: 1.8-mile loop

Approximate hiking time: 1 hour

Trail surface: Forested floor

Difficulty: Easy

Best season: Fall

Other trail users: Trail runners and snowshoers

Canine compatibility: Leashed dogs permitted

Fees and permits: Parking fee charged between May and Oct

Schedule: Open daily year-round, from sunrise to sunset

Maps: USGS Great Barrington; park map available on the park website

Trail contact: Beartown State Forest, 69 Blue Hill Rd., P.O. Box 97, Monterey 01245; (413) 528-0904; www.mass.gov/dcr /parks/western/bear.htm

Finding the trailhead: From the intersection of MA 102 and US 7 in Stockbridge, take US 7 south. Turn left onto Monument Valley Road at 2.6 miles. In 2.0 miles, turn left onto Stony Brook Road. In 2.8 miles, turn left at the sign for Beartown State Forest onto Benedict Pond Road. The trailhead parking area is on the right at 0.4 mile. GPS: N42 12.164' / W73 17.307'

The Hike

From the parking area, head past the map kiosk toward the Benedict Pond shoreline. The Pond Loop Trail starts on

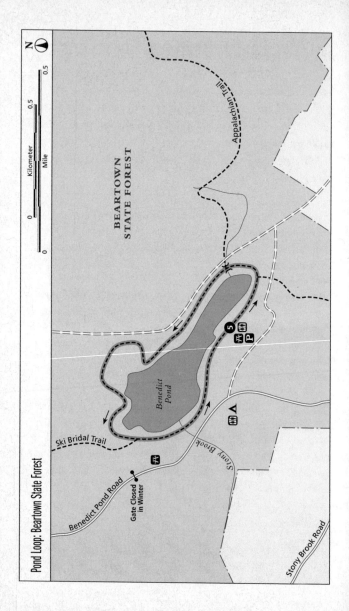

Pond Loop: Beartown State Forest

the right, and the trailhead is well marked. Blue trail markers mark the trail, although I doubt you will need them as the trail is well traveled and easy to follow. It is described traveling counterclockwise.

Keep straight at the junction with the Appalachian National Scenic Trail. The Appalachian Trail, often referred to simply as the AT, is a long-distance hiking trail that starts at Springer Mountain in Georgia and ends at Mount Katahdin in Maine. The AT is approximately 2,178 miles long: Some very serious hikers start in spring with plans to hike the whole trail in one take. They are referred to as thruhikers. For a short while the pond trail will be marked with both white and blue—you are officially on the AT for the white-marked section.

At 0.5 mile turn left, crossing the bridge. The AT leaves to the right; continue straight to stay on track, following the blue trail markers.

The trail turns left and descends back to the edge of the pond. You will pass a big boulder; water seeping through the rock makes this section very icy in the winter months. Come to a beaver hut at 0.9 mile; a bench near the hut makes a great place to take a break. Feel free to leave a note in the Pond Loop note box.

Just after the bench, the trail bends sharply to the right and leaves the edge of the pond. Mountain laurel is abundant on this section of trail. Keep straight at the junction with the Ski Bridal Trail, then pass a campground and cross over the campground access road. The trail bends to the left where the pipeline crosses Stony Brook. Pass the Benedict Pond spillway and head up the stairs to the pond's edge. Turn right and continue over the bridge crossing the spillway.

Follow the edge of the pond, passing the picnic area and bathrooms (open seasonally). The trail reenters the woods near the beach behind the bathrooms. Continue through the picnic area and end at the parking lot and trailhead.

Miles and Directions

0.0 Start from the parking area off Benedict Pond Road; the trailhead is near the pond's edge past the map kiosk.

0.3 Keep straight at the Appalachian Trail junction.

0.5 Turn left and cross the bridge to stay on the Pond Loop Trail.

0.7 Turn left at the trail junction to keep on Pond Loop Trail.

1.5 Keep straight, crossing over the Ski Bridal Trail.

1.6 Keep straight, crossing over the campground access road.

1.7 Turn left at the exposed pipeline to keep on the Pond Loop Trail.

1.8 Arrive back at the parking area and trailhead off Benedict Pond Road.

6 Rounds Rock: Mount Greylock

This short hike will show you what Mount Greylock has to offer without breaking a sweat. The Rounds Rock Trail takes you through a small boreal spruce bog and blueberry barrens, passing the site of a 1948 plane crash. Parts of the wreckage remain as a monument to the pilot who died there.

Distance: 1.0-mile loop
Approximate hiking time: 1 hour
Trail surface: Forested trail
Difficulty: Easy
Best season: Fall
Other trail users: Hikers only
Canine compatibility: Leashed dogs permitted
Fees and permits: None
Schedule: Road open sunrise to sunset from late May through Nov 1

Maps: USGS Cheshire; park map also available at the Mount Greylock Visitor Center and on the park website
Trail contact: Mount Greylock Visitor Center, 30 Rockwell Rd., Lanesborough 01237; (413) 499-4262; www.mass.gov/dcr /parks/mtGreylock/index.htm

Finding the trailhead: From the Mount Greylock Visitor Center on Rockwell Road in Lanesborough, head east on Rockwell Road for 3.0 miles toward the Greylock summit. The parking pullout and trailhead are on the right. GPS: N42 35.603' / W73 11.831'

The Hike

The trail for Rounds Rock starts across the road from the parking area, at the crosswalk. The trail is a narrow footpath marked with blue trail markers; it is well traveled and easy to follow. Go a few hundred feet down the trail, then turn right to start the Rounds Rock loop, traveling in a clock-wise direction.

The trail maintains a steady elevation before descending slightly to the site of the plane wreck at 0.4 mile. John Newcomb, a pilot for the Monticello Aircraft Company, crashed on a delivery run for the *New York Daily Mirror* on August 12, 1948. Hunters discovered the wreckage on December 7, 1948.

From the crash site, the trail continues left, up a small hill. At the top the forest opens up, revealing a boreal spruce bog with blueberry bushes lining the trail. This landscape is not typical for southern New England. At 0.5 mile, keep straight, staying on Rounds Rock Trail. The Northrup Trail leaves to the right. Just a couple hundred feet past this junction, a very short side trail to the right runs down to an overlook. From the overlook gaze westerly to the Catskills of New York and the wind turbines atop Brodie Mountain.

After returning from the vista, turn right to stay on track. The trail continues to wind through the low-lying bushes to another overlook. Again, a side trail leaves to the right to bring you to the vista. Looking south, you have a wonderful view of the Berkshire Hills.

Returning from the vista, turn right to continue on the Rounds Rock Trail. The trail bends to the left and reenters the forest, passing a granite marker; this is the town boundary marker for the towns of New Ashford and Cheshire. At 0.9 mile close the loop, keeping straight at the junction and following the trail back to the parking area and trailhead.

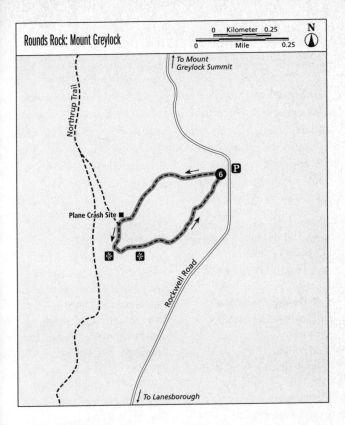

0   Kilometer   0.25

0   Mile   0.25

N

To Mount
Greylock Summit

Northrup Trail

6   P

Plane Crash Site

Rockwell Road

To Lanesborough

Miles and Directions

0.0   Start from the crosswalk on Rockwell Road. After a few hundred feet, turn right to travel the loop in a clockwise direction.

0.5   Keep straight on the Rounds Rock Trail; the Northrup Trail goes right.

0.9   Close the loop, keeping straight on the Rounds Rock Trail.

1.0   Finish at the parking area and trailhead.

7 Ashuwillticook Rail Trail

The Ashuwillticook (ash-oo-will-ti-cook) Rail Trail is a former railroad corridor converted by the Massachusetts Department of Recreation and Conservation into a paved multiuse trail. This 10.9-mile point-to-point trek has plenty of places to rest and picnic along the way. Enjoy views of the Mount Greylock Range across the Cheshire Reservoir. Informative signs will teach you about the area.

Distance: 10.9 miles point to point; bus shuttle or car drop-off required.
Approximate hiking time: 4 to 5 hours
Trail surface: Paved trail
Difficulty: Moderate due to distance
Best season: Fall
Other trail users: Runners, bicyclists, inline skaters, and cross-country skiers
Canine compatibility: Leashed dogs permitted

Fees and permits: None
Schedule: Open daily year-round, from sunrise to sunset
Maps: USGS Cheshire and Pittsfield East; park map available at Berkshire Visitor Center in Adams
Trail contact: Massachusetts Department of Conservation and Recreation, Western Region, P.O. Box 1433/740 South St., Pittsfield 01202; (413) 442-8928; www.mass.gov/dcr/parks /western/asrt.htm

Finding the trailhead: From the intersection of MA 8 and MA 9 in Pittsfield, take MA 8 north for 1.5 miles. At the sign for the Berkshire Mall, turn left. The trailhead and parking area are on the right. GPS: N42 29.348' / W73 12.225'

The Hike

From the parking area, the Ashuwillticook Rail Trail starts at the trailhead bathrooms (open seasonally during daylight hours) and heads north. This rail trail is multiuse, so keep an eye out for cyclists, runners, and people on skates. Most of the trail runs alongside MA 8, but is far enough away to remain mostly peaceful.

The trail passes Berkshire Pond and crosses Nobodys Road. The next 2.5 miles of the trail follow the shore of the Cheshire Reservoir. The trail passes the Farnam's Crossing parking area at 3.7 miles, along the bank of the reservoir. This section of trail is the most beautiful, with amazing views of the Greylock Range across the reservoir. Benches and picnic tables line the trail along the shoreline.

At the north edge of the Cheshire Reservoir, at 5.2 miles, the rail trail crosses MA 8. A traffic light allows for a safe crossing. The trail enters a residential neighborhood. Cross a bridge over the Hoosic River at Harbor Road. Road access and the slow-moving current make this a very popular fishing spot for the locals.

The trail continues to follow the Hoosic River, and the river current gets faster after you pass a small dam. The trail crosses a bridge over the Hoosic as you start to head into the town of Adams. Continue past the Russell Street Field, which offers parking, a playground, tennis courts, and a baseball field. The trail continues into Adams, crossing many busy side streets, before arriving at the Berkshire Visitors Bureau.

A public bus shuttle is available from Center Street in Adams back to the Berkshire Mall. Contact the Berkshire

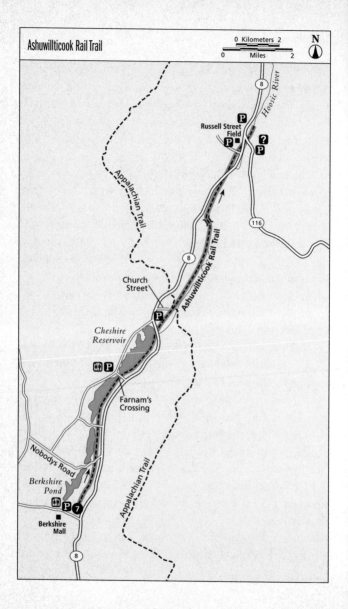

Regional Transit Authority at (800) 292-BRTA or visit www.berkshirerta.com for more information.

Miles and Directions

0.0   Start from the parking area off MA 8.

2.3   Cross Nobodys Road at the south end of Cheshire Reservoir.

3.7   Pass the Farnam's Crossing parking area.

5.2   Cross MA 8 at the north end of Cheshire Reservoir.

5.9   Pass the Church Street parking area and cross the Appalachian Trail.

8.3   Cross the Hoosic River on a bridge at a popular fishing spot.

9.8   Cross the Hoosic River on a bridge.

10.2 Pass the Russell Street Field recreational area.

10.5 Pass the parking area off MA 8 in Adams.

10.9 Arrive at the Berkshire Visitors Bureau and the end of the route.

8 Burbank Trail

The Burbank Trail takes you through one of Berkshire Natural Resources Council's premier properties. This 407–acre parcel is located on the southern slopes of Lenox Mountain. This hike will take you through a beautiful new-growth forest and past the peaceful Monks Pond, an 1800s farmhouse site, and an overlook at the top of the Yokun Ridge.

Distance: 3.2-mile lollipop
Approximate hiking time: 1 to 2 hours
Trail surface: Forested trail
Difficulty: Moderate due to elevation gain
Best season: Fall
Other trail users: Mountain bikers, trail runners, snowshoers, and cross-country skiers
Canine compatibility: Leashed dogs permitted

Fees and permits: None
Schedule: Open daily year-round, from sunrise to sunset
Maps: USGS Stockbridge; park map available on the park website
Trail contact: Berkshire Natural Resources Council, 20 Bank Row, Pittsfield 01201; (413) 499-0596; www.bnrc.net/index .htm

Finding the trailhead: From exit 2 off I-90 (Mass Pike) in Lee, take US 20 west for 4.3 miles. Turn left onto MA 183/Walker Street. In 2.6 miles, turn right onto Richmond Mountain Road. Richmond Mountain Road becomes Lenox Road after 0.9 mile. Continue on Lenox Road for 0.5 mile. Trailhead parking is at Olivia's Overlook. GPS: N42 21.109' / W73 20.263'

The Hike

The Burbank Trail starts at the map kiosk across Lenox Road from the Olivia's Overlook parking area. The hike is marked with red trail markers. Turn right at the junction, following the sign for Monks Pond and traveling the loop in a counterclockwise direction.

The trail is carved into the hillside and follows the lower edge of the Yokun Ridge. At 0.9 mile, pass Monks Pond by keeping straight at the junction; Monks Pond will be to your right. The trail crosses an old stone wall. From the late 1700s into the early 1800s much of this land was cleared to feed the fires required for the iron industry. Stone walls like this one are scattered throughout New England and are a result of land clearing. Most stone walls were used for either property boundaries or animal fencing.

Turn left at the junction with Old Baldhead Road to stay on Burbank Trail. Just after starting the climb, pass the cellar hole of the 1800s John Gorman homestead. As you come to the top of the climb, keep left to continue along the top of the ridge.

At 2.1 miles, a very short spur trail takes you to the Burbank Trail Monument and a nice scenic overlook offering westerly views into the town of Richmond. Continue southwest along the top of the ridge. The trail descends, passing through a clearing made for power lines. Wintergreen and mountain laurel grow in this open space. Continue straight at the junction, closing the loop, to make your way back to the trailhead and parking area at Lenox Road.

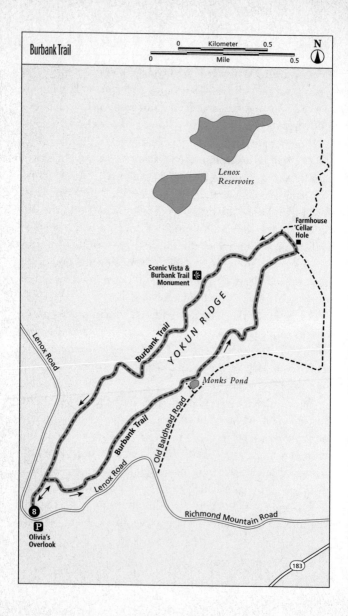

Miles and Directions

0.0 Start at the trailhead across Lenox Road from the Olivia's Overlook parking area.

0.1 Turn right, following the sign for Monks Pond.

0.9 Keep straight at Monks Pond.

1.6 Turn left at the junction with Old Baldhead Road.

1.7 Turn left to stay on the Burbank Trail.

2.1 Arrive at the scenic vista and Burbank Trail Monument. Continue southwest along the ridge.

3.1 Close the loop and keep straight, heading back to the parking area.

3.2 Arrive back at the trailhead and parking area at Olivia's Overlook.

9 Totem Trail: Mohawk Trail State Forest

Mohawk Trail State Forest's 6,800 acres are some of the most scenic woodlands in all of the state. Deep gorges between tall mountains make for some breathtaking scenery. This quick out-and-back takes you to a vista on an unnamed peak that offers great views to the east.

Distance: 2.2 miles out and back

Approximate hiking time: 1 to 2 hours

Trail surface: Forested trail

Difficulty: Moderate

Best season: Fall

Other trail users: Cross-country skiers and snowshoers

Canine compatibility: Leashed dogs permitted

Fees and permits: None

Schedule: Open daily year-round, from sunrise to sunset

Maps: USGS Rowe; park map also available at Mohawk Trail State Forest Campground and on the park website

Trail contact: Mohawk Trail State Forest, 175 Mohawk Trail/Rte. 2, Charlemont; (413) 339-5504; www.mass.gov/dcr/parks/western/mhwk.htm

Finding the trailhead: From the intersection of MA 112 and MA 2 (Mohawk Trail) in Shelburne Falls, take MA 2 west for 12.6 miles. Park in dirt pullout on the right, located after the Mohawk Trail State Forest day-use area. The trailhead is just past the Pioneer Valley sign on MA 2. GPS: N42 38.515' / W72 56.833'

The Hike

From the parking area off MA 2 (Mohawk Trail), head east along MA 2 for 0.1 mile. The trailhead is on the right, just beyond the PIONEER VALLEY sign. Start the hike at the Mohawk Trail State Forest Monument.

Literally just feet after the start of the trail, the Totem Trail turns to the left below the small brown pump house and quickly crosses over two intermittent streams that run side by side. The trail then begins a switchbacking climb through a great second-growth hardwood forest, following blue trail markers. Some of this area was logged in the 1930s, and in the years since has made a great recovery. The trail flattens out as you continue on the path carved into the hillside, crossing over a couple of intermittent steams that only flow with the winter melt and in times of very heavy rain.

At 0.7 mile, the trail turns slightly right, crossing over a wash. This section of trail can be hard to follow, so be alert for blue trail markers. When on a hard-to-follow trail that has markers, if you feel you have "lost" the trail and cannot see any markers ahead, it's a good rule of thumb to look behind you for markers, which will let you know you are on the right track. Trails are generally marked in both directions. If you do fully lose the trail, stay calm, turn around, and retrace your steps until you find the trail again.

Beyond the wash, you start to make the final climb to the rocky outcrop. The trail bends around the east face of an unnamed peak. At 1.1 miles, reach the vista point. The view opens up and offers a glimpse down below to Trout Brook Cove, and east to Hawks Mountain. On a clear day,

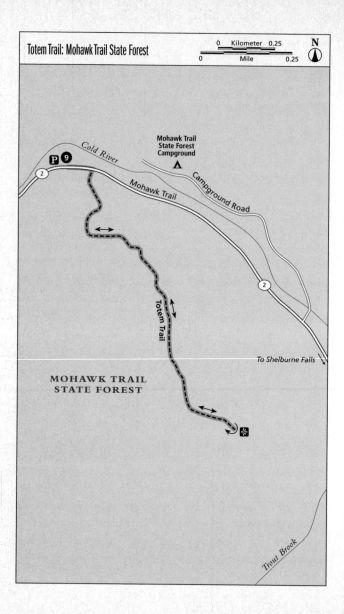

Totem Trail: Mohawk Trail State Forest

0   Kilometer   0.25

0   Mile   0.25

N

Cold River

P 9

2

Mohawk Trail State Forest Campground

Mohawk Trail

Campground Road

2

Totem Trail

To Shelburne Falls

MOHAWK TRAIL STATE FOREST

Trout Brook

Monadnock Mountain in New Hampshire is visible in the far distance. Turn around and retrace your route back to the parking area.

Miles and Directions

0.0 Start from the parking area, heading east along MA 2.

0.1 Reach the start of the Totem Trail, just after the PIONEER VALLEY sign.

0.7 Turn slightly right, crossing a wash easily mistaken for the trail. Follow the blue trail markers.

1.1 Reach the rock outcropping and vista point. Turn around and retrace your route.

2.2 Arrive back at the parking area off MA 2.

10 The Cascades

This short hike is just minutes from downtown North Adams and Williamstown. The Cascades, sometimes referred to as North Brook Falls, are a favorite cool-off spot for the locals, and one of the northern Berkshires' best waterfalls. The North Brook drops over 1,000 feet in 3 miles on its way to the 40-foot cascading falls.

Distance: 1.5 miles out and back

Approximate hiking time: About 1 hour

Trail surface: Forested trail

Difficulty: Easy

Best seasons: Spring and summer

Other trail users: Trail runners

Canine compatibility: Leashed dogs permitted

Fees and permits: None

Schedule: Open daily year-round, from sunrise to sunset

Maps: USGS North Adams

Special considerations: The parking area is in a dense residential neighborhood. The pullout has room for two or three cars at most. Please respect the neighborhood by keeping quiet and not parking or turning around on lawns.

Trail contact: City of North Adams Public Services, 10 Main St., North Adams 01247; (413) 662-3047; www.northadams-ma .gov

Finding the trailhead: From MA 2 in downtown North Adams, head west on MA 2 (West Main Street/Mohawk Trail) for 1.1 miles. Turn left onto Marion Avenue and follow Marion Avenue to its end at 0.1 mile. A parking pullout at the trailhead is on the right. GPS: N42 41.655' / W73 08.121'

The Hike

From the parking area, pass between the wooden fence and the North Brook and follow the well-worn trail southwest. As you leave Marion Avenue and enter the forest the trail widens, following the edge of the brook and climbing gradually. The trail is heavily used but not maintained well; expect to navigate over and around fallen trees.

The trail crosses the North Brook on a secure wooden bridge strong enough to hold up to the rushing winter meltwater. The brook makes its start about 3 miles away in a gorge between Ragged Mountain and Mount Greylock. In early spring, winter snowmelt makes the North Brook a very powerful waterway, depositing boulders downstream and creating small pools for native trout to hide in.

At 0.4 mile, you have to navigate a tricky section where it seems the brook has taken over the trail, especially in times of high water. When the water is low, you can follow the semidry bed a few feet to continue on the trail. When the water is high, it is best to cross the brook, hopping from rock to rock, continue upstream for about 30 feet, then cross back over, rejoining the trail.

You reach the end of the trail at 0.7 mile. If you look upstream into the gorge, you can get a peek at the 40-foot cascading falls. Want a better look? Scramble up the brook into the gorge when the water is low for the best and most refreshing view. Turn around and retrace your steps to return to the parking area.

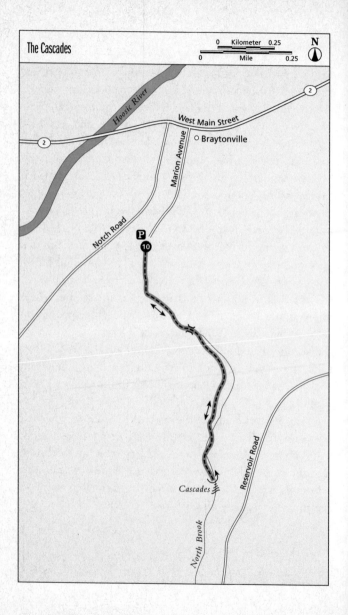

The Cascades

Kilometer
0   0.25
Mile
0   0.25

N

Hoosic River

West Main Street

Braytonville

2

Marion Avenue

Notch Road

P
10

Reservoir Road

Cascades

North Brook

Miles and Directions

0.0 Start the hike from the parking area at the end of Marion Avenue.

0.4 Navigate a tricky section where the stream takes over the trail.

0.75 Arrive at the Cascades, then retrace your route to return.

1.5 Arrive back at the trailhead.

11 Keystone Arches

Hike along a series of dirt roads, jeep trails, and footpaths to the abandoned keystone arch bridges, built in the 1840s and deserted in 1912. Walk along the old rail bed through a hand-dug chasm with 70-foot walls on your way to the last of the arch bridges.

Distance: 4.2 miles out and back

Approximate hiking time: 2 to 3 hours

Trail surface: Forested trail and dirt roads

Difficulty: Easy

Best season: Spring for best view of arches

Other trail users: Mountain bikers, off-road vehicles, equestrians, and snowshoers

Canine compatibility: Leashed dogs permitted

Fees and permits: None

Schedule: Open year-round from sunrise to sunset

Maps: USGS Chester and Becket; park map also available on the park website

Trail contact: Keystone Arches, P.O. Box 276, Huntington 01050; http://keystonearches .org

Finding the trailhead: From the intersection of MA 8 and US 20 in Becket, take US 20 east for 4.2 miles. Turn left onto Middlefield Road. The trailhead and parking area are at 2.6 miles. GPS: N42 18.685' / W72 59.559'

The Hike

The keystone arches were built by hand in the 1840s without mortar. They are the oldest bridges of their kind built for rail use in the United States. The Keystone Arch Bridges Trail, also known as the K.A.B. Trail, is marked with blue trail markers and K.A.B. tags.

From the parking area head north down the dirt road, crossing a metal bridge over a small unnamed brook. Just past the bridge, looking south down the Westfield River, you see a glimpse of the first of the arches. This bridge is the only double-arch bridge in the area.

Turn right, staying on the dirt road. The road follows along a typical New England stone wall. At the break in the wall, turn right onto the footpath, staying on the K.A.B. Trail. The trail winds its way through the woods to the two arches that were abandoned in the 1912 track relocation. These arches were not easy to reach before this trail was built to access them.

At 0.9 mile you come to a keystone arches informational sign telling about the wildlife in the area. Continue on the trail past the sign, and turn right onto the jeep trail. In a couple of hundred feet the jeep trail bends to the right; keep straight onto the footpath to stay on track. You cross a footbridge over a gorge. The footpath meets back up with a jeep trail. Turn right onto the jeep trail.

At 1.6 miles you come to a T junction. A few hundred feet to the left is Keystone Bridge B. Continue right at the junction to reach Keystone Bridge A; this section of trail was the old railway before the relocation. To the left, from the top of the impressive hand-built retaining wall, you have views of a deep gorge through which the west branch of the Westfield River runs. Pass through a massive man-made chasm with 70-foot-high walls. Workers only had picks, shovels, and gunpowder to dig out this chasm for train passage. In winter the walls become covered with ice, making an impressive winter wonderland.

At 2.1 miles you reach Keystone Bridge A, the tallest of all the arches, at 70 feet. Arches A and B are a bit of a tease

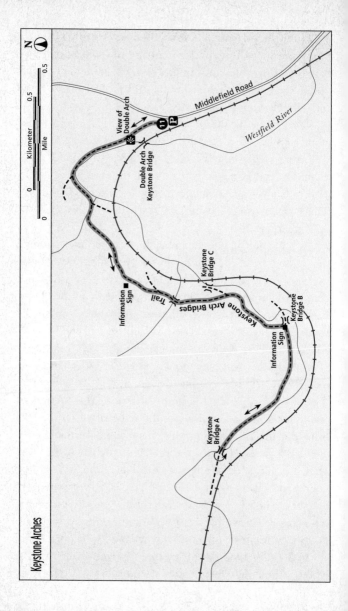

Keystone Arches

because no side trails run to their bases, so you have to settle for the view from atop these architectural wonders.

From Keystone Bridge A, turn around and retrace your route back to the parking area.

Miles and Directions

0.0 Start from the parking area off Middlefield Road by heading north on the dirt road.

0.6 Turn right onto a dirt road, staying on the K.A.B. Trail.

0.8 Turn right onto the footpath at the break in the stone wall.

1.0 Turn right onto the jeep trail, then in 200 feet keep straight onto the footpath.

1.3 Turn right onto the jeep trail.

1.6 Turn right at the T junction, continuing on the jeep trail.

2.1 Reach Keystone Bridge A. From here, turn around and retrace your route to the parking area.

4.2 Arrive back at the trailhead off Middlefield Road.

12 Stony Ledge: Mount Greylock

Stony Ledge is a challenging hike with great views—some say the best views in the Mount Greylock State Reservation. From Stony Ledge you can look up at the summit of Mount Greylock and get a unique view of Massachusetts's highest peak. A short side trip takes you to Greylock's premier waterfall.

Distance: 5.3-mile lollipop
Approximate hiking time: 3 to 4 hours
Trail surface: Dirt road and forested trails
Difficulty: More challenging due to length and elevation gain
Best seasons: Spring and fall
Other trail users: Mountain bikers
Canine compatibility: Leashed dogs permitted

Fees and permits: None
Schedule: Open daily year-round, from sunrise to sunset
Maps: USGS North Adams; park map also available at the Mount Greylock Visitor Center and on the park website
Trail contact: Mount Greylock Visitor Center, 30 Rockwell Rd., Lanesborough 01237; (413) 499-4262; www.mass.gov/dcr /parks/mtGreylock/index.htm

Finding the trailhead: From the intersection of US 7 and MA 43 in Williamstown, take US 7 south for 1.6 miles. Turn left onto Roaring Brook Road. The trailhead and parking area are on the left in 1.0 mile. GPS: N42 38.297' / W73 13.236'

The Hike

From the parking area head southeast to the Roaring Brook trailhead. The trail starts by crisscrossing the Roaring Brook a few times on well-built footbridges to avoid leaving the public property of the state park.

To start the loop portion of the trail, described in a clockwise direction, turn left onto Stony Ledge Ski Trail and start the 1,500-foot climb to Stony Ledge. The Stony Ledge Trail was a ski trail cut by the Civilian Conservation Corps, but is no longer maintained as a ski trail. It is marked with blue trail markers and climbs steeply.

Keep straight at the Haley Farm Trail junction to remain on the Stony Ledge Trail. You will pass an overnight lean-to shelter on the final push to the Stony Ledge lookout at 2.3 miles. The Stony Ledge lookout area is just a tad developed: Scattered around are a few picnic tables, benches, and a composting outhouse. Most prefer to sit on the rock that gives the ledge its name. From the overlook, looking east you can see the war monument atop Mount Greylock, Massachusetts's highest peak. Also within view are Mount Fitch, Mount Williams, and Mount Prospect.

From Stony Ledge, continue southwest heading down Sperry Road, a dirt road now closed to motor vehicles. You pass through the Mount Greylock campground, a hike-in-only campground. Campsites can be reserved at the park website. At the four-way intersection near the campground signboard, turn right, then follow the road to the left. Continue onto the Circle Trail, which leads to Roaring Brook Trail. **Side trip:** Turning left at the four-way trail junction takes you on a 1.0-mile round-trip trek to March Cataract Falls. At 30 feet, it is Mount Greylock's premier waterfall.

Circle Trail will cross two footbridges before you turn right onto Roaring Brook Trail and start your steep descent to the parking area. The Roaring Brook is just out of sight

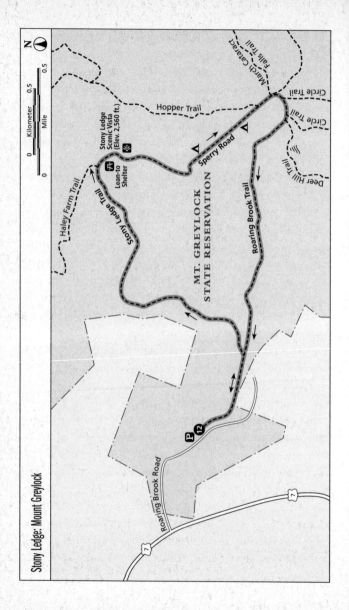

Stony Ledge: Mount Greylock

N

0   0.5   Kilometer
0   0.5   Mile

Haley Farm Trail

Stony Ledge Scenic Vista
(Elev. 2,560 ft.)

Lean-to Shelter

Stony Ledge Trail

Hopper Trail

Sperry Road

MT. GREYLOCK
STATE RESERVATION

Roaring Brook Trail

Circle Trail

Circle Trail

March Cataract
Falls Trail

Deer Hill Trail

P 12

Roaring Brook Road

7

7

from the trail, but when the water is flowing strong, you can hear it.

At the end of the loop you have to cross a small stream, hopping rock-to-rock. Continue straight on Roaring Brook Trail at the junction with Stony Ledge Ski Trail, closing the loop. Follow Roaring Brook Trail, crisscrossing the brook, back to the trailhead and parking area.

Miles and Directions

0.0 Start from the parking area off Roaring Brook Road.

0.5 Turn left onto Stony Ledge Ski Trail.

2.1 Keep straight on Stony Ledge Ski Trail at the junction with Haley Farm Trail.

2.3 Arrive at Stony Ledge. Continue southwest down Sperry Road.

3.3 Turn right onto a dirt road at the four-way intersection near the campground information sign, then follow the road as it bends to the left.

3.4 Turn right onto Circle Trail.

3.5 Turn right onto Roaring Brook Trail at the junction with Deer Hill Trail.

4.8 Keep straight on Roaring Brook Trail at the junction with Stony Ledge Ski Trail, closing the loop.

5.3 Arrive back at the trailhead.

13 Stevens Glen

Well-marked trails lead you on a gentle trek to the iron viewing platform overlooking Stevens Glen. On your way to the glen, pass wildflowers and wild berries on the short journey through the forest.

Distance: 1.2-mile loop
Approximate hiking time: Less than 1 hour
Trail surface: Forested trails
Difficulty: Easy
Best season: Spring
Other trail users: Snowshoers
Canine compatibility: Leashed dogs permitted
Fees and permits: None

Schedule: Open daily year-round, from sunrise to sunset
Maps: USGS Stockbridge; park map available on the park website
Trail contact: Berkshire Natural Resources Council, 20 Bank Row, Pittsfield 01201; (413) 499-0596; www.bnrc.net

Finding the trailhead: From the intersection of US 7 and US 20 in Lenox, take Walker Street northwest for 1.0 mile. Continue straight onto West Street, continuing for 1.6 miles. Turn right onto Richmond Mountain Road, which becomes Lenox Road after 1.6 miles. Turn right onto Lenox Branch Road. The parking pullout and trailhead are on right at 0.3 mile. GPS: N42 21.030' / W73 20.894'

The Hike

From the parking pullout head north, down the stairs and past the map kiosk. The hike is a loop, with spur trails getting you to the start of the loop and to the glen. The trail-head spur winds its way to a junction at the start of the loop, which is traveled in a counterclockwise direction. Turn right, following the red rectangle trail markers.

The trail is well traveled, maintained, and easy to follow. Hemlock, red oak, and pine are plentiful in this part of the forest. The trail crosses a small brook on a footbridge before passing under some power lines. In the clearing for the power lines, wild raspberries and wildflowers grow.

The trail continues through a mixed pine forest, descending slightly and crossing another small brook on a footbridge. Just after the bridge, at the junction, turn right onto the spur trail that brings you to the glen. The trail crosses two brooks on footbridges, the second being Lenox Mountain Brook.

After the second brook, the trail starts to climb to the glen's viewing platform. Rock stairs have been built in the steeper sections to make the climb easier. At the top of the climb you can see the metal stairs leading down to the viewing platform overlooking Stevens Glen.

Lenox Mountain Brook flows through the glen, creating 40-foot cascading falls. Please stay on the trail and viewing platform, as the steep slopes have fragile vegetation that, when disturbed, are susceptible to quick erosion.

From the platform, retrace your steps to the junction by the footbridge. Turn right, following the red triangle trail markers, to resume the loop. The trail continues to climb, passing under the power lines again. At the trail junction, turn right onto the spur trail heading back to the trailhead and parking area.

Miles and Directions

0.0 Start from the parking pullout on Lenox Branch Road.

0.1 Turn right, following the red rectangle trail markers to start the loop.

0.5 Turn right onto the spur trail heading to the glen.

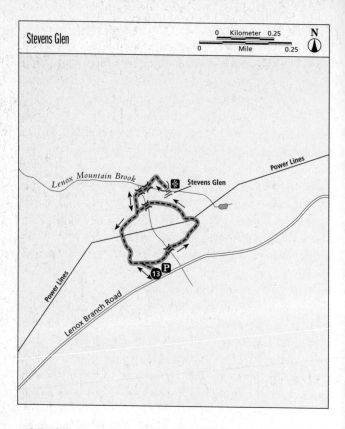

Stevens Glen

0   Kilometer   0.25

0   Mile   0.25

N

Power Lines

Lenox Mountain Brook

Stevens Glen

Power Lines

13 **P**

Lenox Branch Road

0.7 Arrive at the Stevens Glen viewing platform. Retrace your route to the start of the spur trail.

0.9 At the junction, turn right to resume the loop, following the red triangle trail markers.

1.1 Turn right at the junction to return to the parking area.

1.2 Arrive back at the trailhead.

14 Canoe Meadows Wildlife Sanctuary

Just minutes from downtown Pittsfield, Canoe Meadows offers a true wilderness feel. A very popular bird-watching spot in the Berkshires, hike along the Sackett Brook and view wildlife from the observation building on the edge of a beaver marsh.

Distance: 1.8-mile lollipop
Approximate hiking time: Less than 1 hour
Trail surface: Forested trails, grass paths, and cart roads
Difficulty: Easy
Best season: Fall
Other trail users: Trail runners, cross-country skiers, and snowshoers
Canine compatibility: Dogs not permitted
Fees and permits: Fee requested: Place in "on-your-honor" fee box

Schedule: Open Tues through Sun, from 7 a.m. to dusk
Maps: USGS Pittsfield East; park map available on the park website
Trail contact: Mass Audubon, 208 South Great Rd., Lincoln 01773; (413) 637-0320; www .massaudubon.org/Nature_ Connection/Sanctuaries/Canoe_ Meadows/index.php

Finding the trailhead: From the intersection of US 7 and US 20 in Pittsfield, take East Housatonic Street east for 0.2 mile. Turn right onto Pomeroy Avenue. Travel 1.3 miles on Pomeroy Avenue and turn left onto Holmes Road. In 0.2 mile the trailhead and parking area will be on the right. GPS: N42 25.833' / W73 14.258'

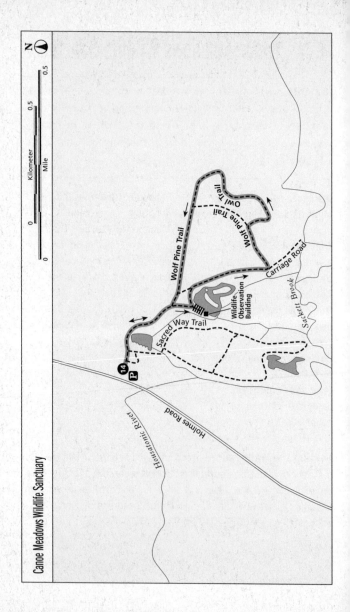

Canoe Meadows Wildlife Sanctuary

The Hike

Head southeast from the parking area, following Carriage Road. Carriage Road passes West Pond, then bends to the right, following along the edge of Sackett Brook. Turn right, following the sign for the observation building; a wooden boardwalk leads you into the building.

The observation building is built on the bank of a marshy beaver wetland. Looking out the small windows of the building, you can see bullfrogs, turtles, muskrats, otters, and tons of bird varieties. The sanctuary is a popular bird-watching spot; more than 150 different birds have been identified here.

Return to the start of the boardwalk and turn right onto the grass path to head back to the carriage road. Continue straight onto the carriage road, traveling the loop portion of the hike in a counterclockwise direction. Beaver wetlands line both sides of the road.

At 0.7 mile, turn left onto Wolf Pine Trail just as the carriage road enters a field of wildflowers. The Wolf Pine Trail leaves the marshy land for a thick forest. At the junction with the Owl Trail, turn right. Follow the Owl Trail, bending along the backside of the property and meeting back up with the Wolf Pine Trail.

Keep straight to continue onto the Wolf Pine Trail. This section of trail runs along an old property line. Metal fence posts still stand, but the fencing has been removed to allow wildlife to roam free.

At 1.5 miles turn right onto the carriage road and follow it back to the trailhead and parking area.

Miles and Directions

0.0 From the parking area, head southeast on Carriage Road.

0.2 Turn right onto the trail leading to the observation building.

0.3 Arrive at the observation building. Turn around and return to Carriage Road by turning right at the end of the boardwalk.

0.4 Keep straight on Carriage Road.

0.7 Turn left onto the Wolf Pine Trail.

0.8 Turn right onto the Owl Trail.

1.2 Keep straight onto the Wolf Pine Trail.

1.5 Turn right onto Carriage Road.

1.8 Arrive back at the trailhead.

15 Tannery Falls

Savoy Mountain State Forest was created in 1918 with the purchase of 1,000 acres of farmland. Hike through old farmland reforested in the 1930s. The big reward is Tannery Falls, a 100-foot cascading waterfall. Return along pristine Ross Brook and take an optional side trip to Balanced Rock.

Distance: 4.7-mile loop with a spur to the waterfall
Approximate hiking time: 3 to 4 hours
Trail surface: Dirt road and forested trails
Difficulty: Moderate due to length
Best season: Spring
Other trail users: Mountain bikers, snowmobilers, and snowshoers
Canine compatibility: Leashed dogs permitted

Fees and permits: None
Schedule: Open daily year-round, from sunrise to sunset
Maps: USGS Windsor and North Adams; park map also available at Savoy Mountain Campground and on the park website
Trail contact: Savoy Mountain State Forest, 260 Central Shaft Rd., Florida 01247; (413) 663-8469; www.mass.gov/dcr/parks/western/svym.htm

Finding the trailhead: From the intersection of MA 8 and MA 116 in Adams, take MA 8 (Park Street) north for 0.4 mile. Turn right onto Hoosac Street. Hoosac Street becomes Upper East Hoosac Street, then Adams Road. Turn left onto New State Road. Roadside parking and the trailhead are on the right in 1.4 miles, at the junction with Tannery Road. GPS: N42 37.419' / W73 02.009'

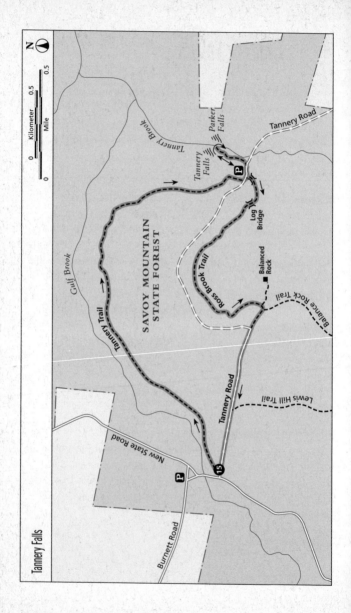

Tannery Falls

The Hike

The Tannery Trail starts on the left and heads northeast from where Tannery Road meets New State Road. The Tannery Trail is an old jeep trail closed to all motorized vehicles except snowmobiles in winter. Unfortunately, some ATV riders break the rule. The Tannery Trail is not well maintained so expect downed trees and wet areas that you will need to navigate carefully. The trail descends slowly through a second-growth forest; the Civilian Conservation Corps reforested much of this area in the 1930s.

At 2.2 miles Tannery Trail junctions with Tannery Road; turn left onto Tannery Road. The dirt road crosses Ross Brook on a bridge built for cars. Just after the bridge turn left into the upper parking area. The trail to the falls starts at the white marker on the far edge of the open parking area.

The blue-marked trail descends quickly along the edge of Ross Brook. Wooden steps and makeshift handrails are in place on some of the steeper sections to make your descent safer and easier. As you reach the base of the stairs, Parker Falls is to the right. Parker on its own is a great destination, but continue straight for a couple of hundred feet to the real prize: Tannery Falls.

Ross Brook gathers at the top of Tannery Falls before dropping nearly 100 feet to the pool at the base. When water flow is good these falls are spectacular, but in the dry times of summer, they can slow to nothing more than a trickle. Turn around and retrace your steps back to Tannery Road.

Across Tannery Road from the parking area, pick up a small spur trail that leads you to Ross Brook Trail for your return. Take the spur trail crossing a wooden slat bridge, then continue straight onto Ross Brook Trail. The trail climbs slightly, following the edge of Ross Brook for most of the return hike (though it leaves the edge at times only to later return).

At 2.9 miles cross a log bridge, and the trail continues to follow the very edge of the brook. The Ross Brook Trail emerges at an unnamed dirt road. Turn right on the dirt road to continue your return. **Side trip:** Turn left onto the dirt road for a 0.2 mile round-trip up to Balanced Rock.

The unnamed road meets up with Tannery Road. Turn left and follow Tannery Road back to the trailhead.

Miles and Directions

0.0 Start on the Tannery Trail, leaving from the junction of Tannery Road and New State Road.

2.2 Turn left onto Tannery Road, then turn left into the upper parking area. The trail to the falls starts at the opposite side of parking area.

2.3 Start the trail to Tannery Falls.

2.5 Arrive at Tannery Falls; retrace your route back to Tannery Road.

2.7 Start the Ross Brook Trail from Tannery Road. The trail begins across the road from the parking area.

2.8 Turn right to stay on Ross Brook Trail.

2.9 Cross Ross Brook on a log bridge.

3.9 Turn right onto the unnamed dirt road.

4.0 Turn left onto Tannery Road.

4.4 Keep straight on Tannery Road; Lewis Hill Trail leaves to the left.

4.7 Arrive at the trailhead at the junction of Tannery Road and New State Road.

16 Ice Glen

Just seconds from downtown Stockbridge, Ice Glen offers a climb through a glacial ravine. Climb over and around rocks and boulders to make your way through the glen. The crevasses of the glen sometimes harbor ice into the summer. At the end of the glen, sit beneath what some argue is the oldest pine tree in the state.

Distance: 1.4 miles out and back

Approximate hiking time: Less than 1 hour

Trail surface: Forested trails

Difficulty: Moderate due to rock scrambling in Ice Glen

Best season: Spring

Other trail users: Only hikers

Canine compatibility: Leashed dogs permitted

Fees and permits: None

Schedule: Open daily year-round, from sunrise to sunset

Maps: USGS Stockbridge; map sign at the trailhead

Trail contact: Laurel Hill Association—Trails, P.O. Box 24, Stockbridge 01262

Finding the trailhead: From the junction of US 7 and MA 102 in Stockbridge, take Main Street (US 7/MA 102) west for 0.4 mile. Turn left onto US 7 (South Street). In 0.2 mile turn left onto Park Street. Park Street ends at the trailhead parking area. GPS: N42 16.708' / W73 18.440'

The Hike

Head southeast from the parking area, crossing the Housatonic River on the Goodrich Memorial Suspension Footbridge. After the footbridge keep straight, crossing the railroad tracks. Mary Flynn Trail leaves to the left. The trail

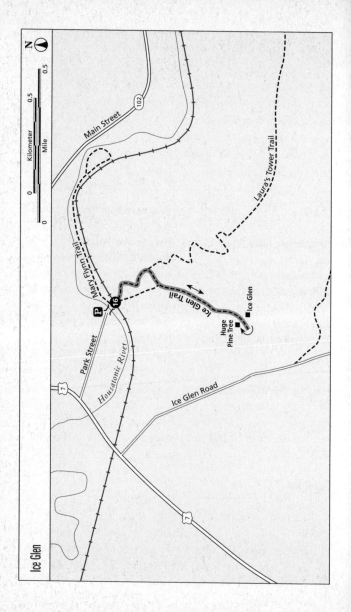

Ice Glen

to Ice Glen starts to climb through a mixed forest just after the tracks. White pine and hemlock trees make up the larger trees in the area. At 0.3 mile turn right, following the sign marked GLEN. (A left turn will take you to Laura's Tower.) The trail winds its way to the mouth of the glen.

At the start of the glen a moss-covered vertical rock face is inscribed ICE GLEN—THE GIFT TO STOCKBRIDGE—OF—DAVID DUDLEY FIELD—1891. If you enter the glen on a hot summer day, you will feel the rush of cold air flowing out from the cracks and crevices deep below. Many large rocks and boulders have fallen from above due to frost and tree root damage. These fallen rocks have created many small passageways and minicaves that adventurous children love to explore. Some of these rocks can be slippery and tricky to climb over, so be cautious. The Ice Glen gets its name because the glen holds ice much longer than anywhere else in the area—sometimes ice can be found in the glen into June.

As you continue, a wood slat bridge crosses to the opposite side of the glen. Before you know it, you reach the end of the glen; it is only 0.2 mile long. At the end, on the left, grows a gigantic white pine estimated to be 300 years old and argued to be the oldest in the state. A bench at the base makes for a good resting point before retracing your steps back to the trailhead.

Miles and Directions

0.0 From the parking area head southeast, crossing the footbridge. Just after the bridge keep straight at the junction with Mary Flynn Trail, crossing the railroad tracks.

0.3 Turn right onto the trail to the glen.

0.4 Turn left at the junction to continue to the glen.

0.5 Reach the start of Ice Glen.

0.7 Reach end of Ice Glen at the huge white pine tree. Retrace your steps to return to the parking area.

1.4 Arrive back at the trailhead.

17 Old Mill Trail

This river walk mixes the natural beauty of the river with the rich history of a business that once thrived here in the Berkshires. This short walk takes you along the river's edge, passing the ruins of a nineteenth-century textile mill, along old penstocks used to divert water to the mills downstream.

Distance: 1.6 miles out and back

Approximate hiking time: Less than 1 hour

Trail surface: Gravel and forested trails

Difficulty: Easy

Best seasons: Spring and fall

Other trail users: Trail runners and snowshoers

Canine compatibility: Leashed dogs permitted

Fees and permits: None

Schedule: Open daily year-round, from sunrise to sunset

Maps: USGS Pittsfield East; park map available on the park website

Trail contact: Housatonic Valley Association, P.O. Box 251/1383 Rte. 102, South Lee 01260; (413) 394-9796; http://hva today.org/

Finding the trailhead: From the junction of MA 8 and MA 9 in Pittsfield, take Main Street (MA 8) south for 2.9 miles. Turn left onto Old Dalton Road. The trailhead and parking area are on the left in 100 feet. GPS: N42 26.877' / W73 07.843'

The Hike

From the parking area head north on the gravel trail. The newly built Old Mill Trail was constructed to minimize damage to the Housatonic's riverbank. The path was completely excavated and gravel was put in place on top of a

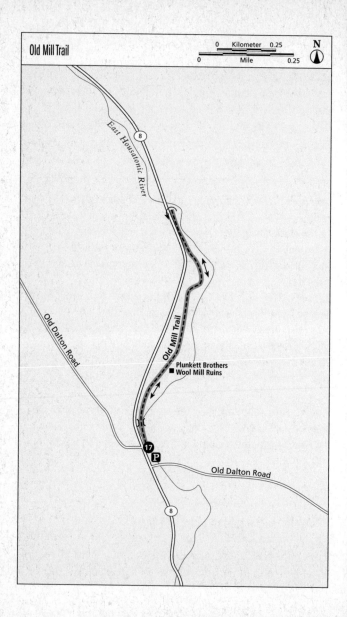

special fabric to resist erosion and keep plant life off the track. Composite bridges were built for safe passage over the river and across drainage ditches.

The trail follows the river's floodplain, a wet environment that makes it easy for many fern species to line the route. At 0.1 mile cross the river on the largest of the bridges—volunteers built this 50-foot bridge in one day.

After passing over two smaller bridges crossing drainage gullies, you come to the remains of a large mill complex that once stood along the river. The dam, penstock, and parts of the foundation are all that remain. A short spur trail turns left and runs along the top of the dam for a different vantage point.

On the north side of the dam, the trail continues straight and the foundation of the Plunkett Brothers Wool Mill can be seen. The path bends sharply to the right, returning to the riverbank, then follows an old penstock that was used to divert water to the mill and turn a wheel to power machinery.

The route ends at MA 8. The Housatonic Valley Association plans to continue the trail as funding allows but for now, you will have to call this its end. Turn around and retrace your route back to the southern trailhead.

Miles and Directions

0.0   Start from the parking area off Old Dalton Road, heading north on the gravel trail.

0.1   Cross the Housatonic River on a bridge.

0.3   Keep straight on the gravel path; a short spur trail leaves to the left along the dam.

0.8   The trail ends at MA 8. Turn around and retrace the route to the trailhead.

1.6   Arrive back at the trailhead.

18 Laura's Tower

Enjoy a three-state view from Laura's Tower. Use the locator wheel atop the tower to orient yourself with area mountain ranges. Climb through stands of old hemlock and white pine that the Laurel Hill Association has been protecting since 1853, making it the oldest conservation group still active today.

Distance: 1.6 miles out and back

Approximate hiking time: Less than 1 hour

Trail surface: Forested trails

Difficulty: Moderate due to elevation gain

Best season: Fall

Other trail users: Snowshoers

Canine compatibility: Leashed dogs permitted

Fees and permits: None

Schedule: Open daily year-round, from sunrise to sunset

Maps: USGS Stockbridge; map sign at the trailhead

Trail contact: Laurel Hill Association–Trails, P.O. Box 24, Stockbridge 01262

Finding the trailhead: From the junction of US 7 and MA 102 in Stockbridge, take Main Street (US 7/MA 102) west for 0.4 mile. Turn left onto US 7 (South Street). In 0.2 mile turn left onto Park Street. Park Street ends at the trailhead and parking area. GPS: N42 16.708' / W73 18.440'

The Hike

Head southeast from the parking area, crossing the Housatonic River on the Goodrich Memorial Suspension Footbridge. After the footbridge, keep straight across the railroad tracks. The Mary Flynn Trail leaves to the left. Continue on the Laura's Tower Trail. The trail starts to climb through a

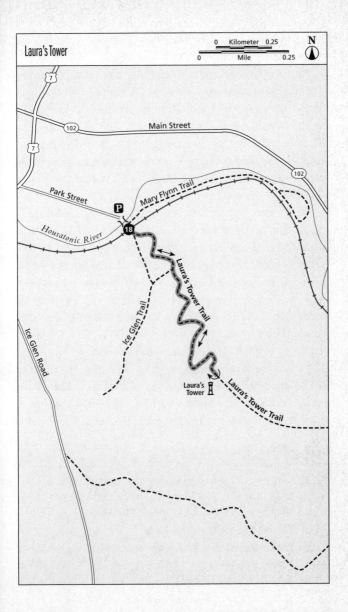

Laura's Tower

0   Kilometer   0.25
0   Mile   0.25

N

Main Street

Park Street

Mary Flynn Trail

Housatonic River

18

Ice Glen Trail

Laura's Tower Trail

Ice Glen Road

Laura's
Tower

Laura's Tower Trail

mixed forest just after the tracks. White pine and hemlock trees make up the larger trees in the area.

At 0.3 mile turn left, following the sign marked TOWER. (Turning right will take you to Ice Glen.) The trail bends to the left through a rock garden of big boulders before starting the switchback climb to the tower. As you get closer to the tower you will notice that less and less of the massive hemlock, ash, and white pine trees are standing. These trees were cleared out for a wide-open view when the tower was built.

At 0.8 mile you will arrive at the tower. The view from the bottom of the tower is nonexistent and climbing the metal tower is not for everyone. But the tower gets you just above the tree line and the view is wonderful—180 degrees from east to west. A "points of interest" wheel atop the tower lets you know what mountains you are looking at and how far away the range is. On a clear day you can see south into Connecticut, west to the New York Catskills, and north to the Green Mountains of Vermont.

Laurel Hill Association built Laura's Tower in 1931 for use as a fire tower. Founded in 1853, Laurel Hill is the country's oldest conservation group still managing land today. From the tower, retrace your steps to the trailhead.

Miles and Directions

0.0 From the parking area head southeast, crossing the footbridge. Just after the bridge keep straight at the junction with Mary Flynn Trail, crossing the railroad tracks.

0.3 Turn left onto the trail to the tower.

0.8 Reach Laura's Tower, then retrace your steps to return to the parking area.

1.6 Arrive back at the trailhead.

19 Bartholomew's Cobble

Hike through fields and forests on this nice route. Pass through beautiful fields of wildflowers on your way to Hurlburt's Hill, a pristine scenic overlook. Stroll along the banks of the Housatonic River, passing the second largest cotton-wood tree in the state. Return on the Ledges Trail, which makes its way around the cobble that gives this property its name.

Distance: 3.8-mile double loop with spur
Approximate hiking time: 1 to 2 hours
Trail surface: Forested trails
Difficulty: Moderate due to climb to Hurlburt's Hill
Best season: Fall
Other trail users: Trail runners, snowshoers, and cross-country skiers
Canine compatibility: Dogs not permitted

Fees and permits: Fee charged at visitor center
Schedule: Open daily year-round, from sunrise to sunset
Maps: USGS Ashley Falls; park map available at the visitor center and on the park website
Trail contact: Bartholomew's Cobble, 105 Weatogue Rd., Sheffield 01257; (413) 229-8600; www.thetrustees.org /places-to-visit/berkshires /bartholomews-cobble.html

Finding the trailhead: From the junction of US 7 and MA 23 in Great Barrington, take MA 23/US 7 (State Road) south for 0.5 mile. Turn left, staying on US 7 south for 8.5 miles. Turn right onto MA 7A (Ashley Falls Road). In 0.5 mile turn right onto Rannapo Road and follow it for 1.6 miles. Turn right at Weatogue Road, a dirt road. The parking area and trailhead are on the left after 0.1 mile. GPS: N42 03.451' / W73 21.044'

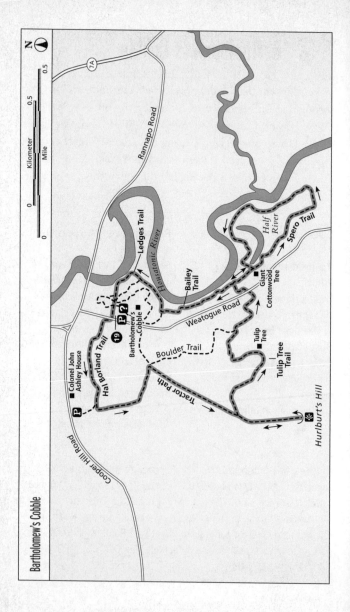

Bartholomew's Cobble

The Hike

From the visitor center parking area, cross Weatogue Road and enter the field. The Hal Borland Trail follows the northern edge of the field. Many different wildflowers grow in the fields and open spaces throughout the year. A sign-board on the outside of the visitor center shows photos of what is in bloom at any given time. The trail bends to the left, following a cow pasture filled with friendly cows that love to come up to the fence to say hi.

At 0.6 mile turn right onto Tractor Path and climb to Hurlburt's Hill. At the high point of the twenty-acre field, benches face north for lovely views of Mount Everett and the Housatonic River valley. Retrace your steps to the trail junction, turning right onto the Tulip Tree Trail. A giant tulip tree that you pass along the trail gives the trail its name. At the next junction turn right to continue descending on Boulder Trail.

The trail crosses over Weatogue Road and descends to the Housatonic River floodplain. Turn right to start the Spero Trail. At the massive cottonwood tree keep right: The loop (traveled counterclockwise) takes you around Half River, which is nothing more than a small pond.

Continue along the banks of the river, returning to the massive cottonwood tree, the second largest in the state. Turn right to keep following the bank of the Housatonic River, cutting through a couple of fields strewn with wildflowers.

At 3.5 miles, turn right onto the Ledges Trail. The Ledges Trail wraps around the outer edge of the cobble that makes this place so unique. The rock faces and cliffs of the cobble line the trail.

Keep on the Ledges Trail, following it back to the visitor center parking area and trailhead.

Miles and Directions

0.0 From the parking area, cross Weatogue Road to start on the Hal Borland Trail, which follows the edge of the field.

0.3 Keep straight at the junction; the trail bends left, following a cow pasture.

0.6 Turn right onto the Tractor Path.

1.4 Arrive at Hurlburt's Hill, then retrace your steps and descend to the Tractor Path.

1.6 Turn right onto the Tulip Tree Trail.

2.0 Turn right onto the Boulder Trail.

2.1 Keep straight, crossing over Weatogue Road.

2.2 Turn right onto the Spero Trail.

2.3 Keep right at the giant cottonwood tree to start the Spero Trail.

2.6 Go slightly left, following the white trail makers, to stay on the Spero Trail.

3.1 Turn right at the giant cottonwood tree and continue to follow the edge of the river.

3.2 Keep straight at the Spero/Boulder Trail junction onto Bailey Trail.

3.5 Turn right onto the Ledges Trail.

3.6 Keep right on the Ledges Trail.

3.8 Arrive back at the trailhead.

20 Dunbar Brook

Hike along the powerful Dunbar Brook, passing many small falls and rapids. Pass through some of the finest old–growth forest in all of New England—some trees along the trail are up to 500 years old and reach 125 feet in height.

Distance: 6.2 miles out and back

Approximate hiking time: 3 to 4 hours

Trail surface: Forested trail

Difficulty: Moderate due to distance and elevation gain

Best season: Fall

Other trail users: Snowshoers

Canine compatibility: Leashed dogs permitted

Fees and permits: None

Schedule: Open daily year-round, from sunrise to sunset

Maps: USGS Rowe; park map available on the park website

Trail contact: Monroe State Forest, Tilda Hill Road, Monroe 01350; (413) 339-5504; www .mass.gov/dcr/parks/western /mnro.htm

Finding the trailhead: From the intersection of MA 2 and MA 8 in North Adams, take MA 2 east for 6.7 miles. Turn left onto Whitcomb Hill Road. In 2.5 miles turn left on River Road. Parking and the trailhead are on the left, across from the Dunbar Brook Picnic Area, at 4.8 miles. GPS: N42 42.269' / W72 57.164'

The Hike

Head southwest from the trailhead, climbing the power line access road. The Dunbar Brook Trail enters the forest about 100 feet up the road on the right. The trail is marked with blue trail markers.

At the start of the trail, the Bear Swamp Hydroelectric Project dams the Dunbar Brook. The New England Power

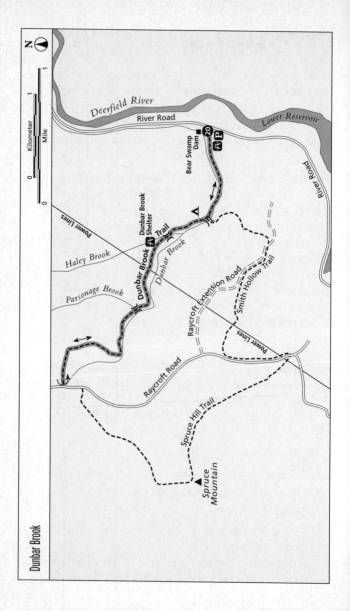

Dunbar Brook

Company worked hard to preserve and enhance recreation opportunities in the area. The Dunbar Brook travels through some intense terrain. The topography of Monroe State Forest has kept loggers out for years. The state forest boasts over 250 acres of the finest old-growth forest in all of southern New England.

At 0.8 mile turn right at the junction with Smith Hollow Trail and cross over the Dunbar Brook on a large wooden bridge. The trail continues to follow the edge of the brook, passing a campsite. This campsite is open to the public and free to use on a first-come, first-served basis. Three overnight shelters, free to use, are also in the forest. This area makes for a great beginner overnight backpacking trip.

The trail crosses over Haley Brook on a wood bridge. Continue behind the Dunbar Brook Shelter and turn right to stay on the Dunbar Brook Trail. You will pass a primitive outhouse on your left. The trail continues to follow the brook, which drops 700 feet in 2 miles and creates many small cascading falls and large pools visible from the trail. Cross Parsonage Brook on a bridge; for a short section you have the Dunbar Brook roaring on your left and Parsonage Brook babbling on your right.

The trail bends to the right at 2.3 miles, starting a climb away from the Dunbar Brook. Pass many large boulders among the old-growth forest. Turn left, descending to stay on track; the trail emerges at Raycroft Road. A large rock along the brook makes for a nice resting point before turning around to retrace your route back to the trailhead and parking area.

Miles and Directions

0.0 From the parking area head southwest on the power line access road. The Dunbar Brook Trail enters on the right.

0.8 Turn right and cross Dunbar Brook.

0.9 Pass the campsite.

1.1 Cross Haley Brook and pass the Dunbar Brook Shelter.

1.5 Pass under power lines.

1.9 Cross Parsonage Brook.

3.0 Turn left, descending to stay on Dunbar Brook Trail.

3.1 Reach Raycroft Road. Turn around and retrace your route back to the parking area.

6.2 Arrive back at the trailhead off River Road.

Clubs and Trail Groups

Appalachian Mountain Club: Berkshire Chapter; 5 Joy St., Boston 02108; (800) 372-1758; www.amcberkshire.org. For over eighty years, the Berkshire chapter has promoted the protection, enjoyment, and wise use of the mountains, rivers, and trails in the Berkshires.

Pioneer Valley Hiking Club; www.pioneervalleyhiking club.org. The club promotes outdoor activities centered around New England for over 200 members.

Sierra Club: Massachusetts Chapter; 10 Milk St., Suite 632, Boston 02108; (617) 423-5775; www.sierraclubmass .org. Since 1892, the Sierra Club has been working to protect communities, wild places, and the planet itself.

About the Author

Jim Bradley grew up on the outskirts of Western, Massachusetts. Growing up, Jim spent many years as a Boy Scout. As a Scout, he learned to respect nature and fell in love with the outdoors. Jim has spent the last fifteen years hiking and exploring the hills of Western and the Berkshires.

Jim now lives in Northampton, Massachusetts, and is the sole author of his outdoor blog: http://huskyhiker.com. He still spends time exploring the trails of New England. Jim enjoys camping, kayaking, geocaching, and bicycling when he is not hiking.

WHAT'S SO SPECIAL ABOUT UNSPOILED, NATURAL PLACES?

Beauty   Solitude   Wildness   Freedom   Quiet   Adventure
Serenity   Inspiration   Wonder   Excitement
Relaxation   Challenge

There's a lot to love about our treasured public lands, and the reasons are different for each of us. Whatever your reasons are, the national **Leave No Trace** education program will help you discover special outdoor places, enjoy them, and preserve them—today and for those who follow. By practicing and passing along these simple principles, you can help protect the special places you love from being loved to death.

THE PRINCIPLES OF **LEAVE NO TRACE**

- Plan ahead and prepare
- Travel and camp on durable surfaces
- Dispose of waste properly
- Leave what you find
- Minimize campfire impacts
- Respect wildlife
- Be considerate of other visitors

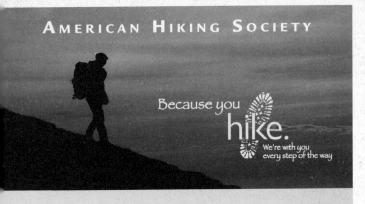

To discover more outdoor adventures near you, check out these other great FalconGuides:

Hiking Vermont

Best Easy Day Hikes Albany

Best Hikes Near Boston

Hiking Massachusetts

Hiking Southern New England

Road Biking Massachusetts

Best Rail Trails New England

Hiking New Hampshire